Weather Watchers

COLD

WRITTEN BY
E.C. Andrews

KidHaven
PUBLISHING

Published in 2025 by
KidHaven Publishing, an Imprint of
Greenhaven Publishing, LLC
2544 Clinton St., Buffalo, NY 14224

Written by: E.C. Andrews
Edited by: Rebecca Phillips-Bartlett
Designed by: Amelia Harris

Cataloging-in-Publication Data

Names: Andrews, E.C.
Title: Cold / E.C. Andrews.
Description: Buffalo, New York : KidHaven Publishing, 2025. | Series: Weather watchers | Includes glossary and index.
Identifiers: ISBN 9781534547346 (pbk.) | ISBN 9781534547353 (library bound) | ISBN 9781534547360 (ebook)
Subjects: LCSH: Cold--Juvenile literature. | Temperature--Juvenile literature. | Weather--Juvenile literature.
Classification: LCC QC981.3 A537 2025 | DDC 551.5'25--dc23

Manufactured in the United States of America

CPSIA compliance information: Batch #CSKH25
For further information contact Greenhaven Publishing LLC at 1-844-317-7404.

Please visit our website, www.greenhavenpublishing.com.
For a free color catalog of all our high-quality books, call toll free 1-844-317-7404 or fax 1-844-317-7405.

Find us on

IMAGE CREDITS

All images are courtesy of Shutterstock.com, unless otherwise specified. With thanks to Getty Images, Thinkstock Photo and iStockphoto.
Cover – Oleh Svetiukha, baldezh, Heleno4ka, Virtis, Volha Valadzionak, Ingrid Maasik, kzww, Rashid Valitov, Ondrej Prosicky, Character – Andrew Rybalko. 2–3 – avtk, Virtis. 4–5 – Leigh Prather, solarseven, Hakase_420, Krushevskaya, maljuk. 6–7 – yaruna, PremiumArt, LadadikArt, Kirill Gorshkov, Sensvector. 8–9 – Zaitsava Olga, AlanVec, Ingrid Maasik, Bargais, mentalmind. 10–11 – Olya Humeniuk, YummyBuum, avtk, desigerxx, mentalmind, Milya Shaykh. 12–13 – Krasula, GoodStudio, AlexanderTrou, Vitalii Bashkatov, Amado Designs. 14–15 – poltu shyamal, Andrey Arkusha, Krushevskay, mentalmind. 16–17 – Scherbinator, Frederic Legrand - COMEO, Virtis, Arcady, Dmitriy Kochergin, Sensvector. 18–19 – zedspider, Ivan Dubovik, Galliina, HeyDebbie. 20–21 – Lana Sham, Prostock-studio, stockakia. 22–23 – Pressmaster, Oleon17, Milya Shaykh, Ground Picture.

CONTENTS

Words that look like this can be found in the glossary on page 24.

WHAT IS WEATHER?

Welcome to Weather Watchers TV, folks. My name is Devin. I am reporting from somewhere that is very cold. Before we get into that, let's talk about what is making it so cold.

The weather is what you see and feel when you go outside. It can be sunny, windy, or stormy. I am knee-deep in snow, so I will report what happens when the weather turns cold.

COLD WEATHER

It is pretty cool where I am, in more ways than one! This is because the part of the planet I am on is facing away from the sun. This makes the weather colder.

If you live somewhere that gets very cold, it is important to dress warm. Thermal clothes and waterproof coats are must-haves for playing outside in that cold winter weather.

SNOW AND ICE

Snow comes from clouds. Normally, clouds are full of tiny drops of water. When clouds get very cold, these waterdrops freeze. The frozen water droplets stick together and fall to the ground as snowflakes.

Unlike snow, ice needs something solid to freeze onto. When it is cold enough, water that is on hard surfaces will freeze solid. Next time it is cold, count how many frozen puddles you see.

WINTER FUN

It may be a bit chilly, but winter can be a wonderful time of year. There are lots of fun things to do. If it snows, you could build snowmen or go sledding.

The world outside changes when it gets cold. Why not take a cold-weather walk and see what has changed since summer? Do the trees still have their leaves? Can you spot any winter wildlife?

STAYING SAFE

Ice is slippery stuff. It can make roads dangerous to drive on. Salt trucks are used to make roads safer. These big machines spread salt across the road. Salt helps to melt the ice.

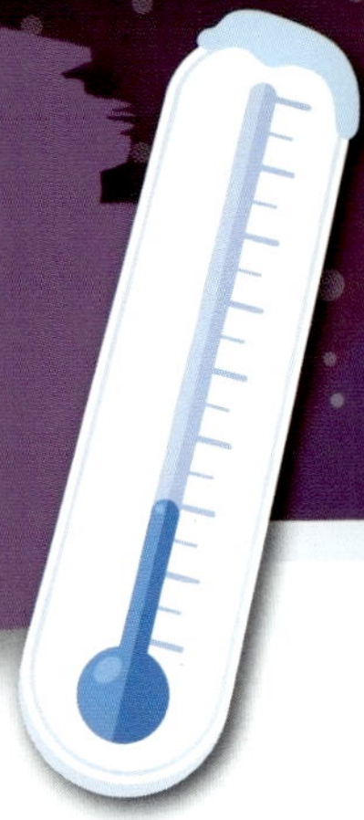

Winter boots are made to have a good grip on slippery surfaces.

In some places, it gets dark early in the winter. This is because Earth is facing away from the sun. Some countries also put the clocks back by one hour during fall and winter.

FEELING CHILLY?

Have you ever wondered why we shiver when we are cold? We shiver because our bodies are trying to warm up. Shivering happens when your muscles tighten and relax very quickly over and over again.

When it is cold enough to shiver, you might also see your breath in the air. This is because your breath has tiny drops of water in it that create a little cloud when they get cold.

CHILLY DISASTERS

As wonderful as snow can be, sometimes it can get a bit out of hand! When lots of snow gets paired with strong winds, a snowstorm happens. Very strong snowstorms are called blizzards.

Blizzards can cause car accidents because they make it very difficult to see. The wind and heavy snow can cause trees to fall. Blizzards can cause floods when the snow melts.

HYPOTHERMIA

Hypothermia is when you get so cold that your body cannot work properly. Hypothermia can make you feel confused or tired. Someone with hypothermia might shiver a lot. They might have trouble breathing and talking.

Hypothermia does not happen easily, but it is always important to stay safe. Always be sure to wear warm clothes in cold weather and never go into icy water.

WINTER NIBBLES

Too cold to go outside? Why not sit inside with a blanket, a book, and a nice cup of your favorite hot drink? You could even watch the winter weather from the window. How cozy!

Hot soups, stews, and casseroles are good meals to warm you up. You can make so many different kinds. No matter what your favorite foods are, there is a soup out there for you!

You could even invent a new flavor of soup!

SAFE AND SNUG

Being chilly should not stop you from being cheerful. Cold weather can bring some wonderful things. As long as you stay safe, there is lots of fun to be had.

Grab your winter coat and boots and have some warm food at the ready. Your winter wonderland awaits! I am Devin. Thank you for tuning into Weather Watchers TV!

We will see you next time!

GLOSSARY

FLOOD when an area has more water than usual

FREEZE to harden into ice or become hard from cold temperatures

GRIP the ability to hold on to another thing well

MUSCLE a bundle of tissue inside the body that can contract or squeeze together

SOLID firm and stable, not a liquid

SURFACE the outside layer of something

THERMAL something that stays warm by trapping heat inside it

INDEX